May you find a blessing here.

Debbie

D0043052

Amazon.com/author/debbie woods

Mended: Out of the Rag Pile, Back on the Hanger

Published by
HigherLife Publishing & Marketing Inc.
PO Box 623307
Oviedo, FL 32762
www.ahigherlife.com

Scripture quotations, unless otherwise noted, are from the Revised Standard Version (RSV), 1952. Used by permission.

Paperback ISBN: 978-0-9978018-4-2
ebook ISBN: 978-0-9978018-5-9

Cover design: Bill Johnson

First Edition
16 17 18 19 20 21 — 9 8 7 6 5 4 3 2 1
Printed in the United States of America

Praise for Mended

"This anointed book will change the way you see the world. Debbie shows us how to intimately notice and experience the hand of God. It changes an ordinary life to an extraordinary life of awe."

David L. Cook, PhD
Author, *Seven Days in Utopia: Golf's Sacred Journey*

"I'm tellin' you, this is one fantastic lady who reflects her trust in God through this book. Through tough times (and I mean really tough times) she is able to laugh at herself and with God. These devotions made me laugh and cry but always brought me back to the amazing God we serve, like a box of really good chocolates that you want to eat all at once but limit yourself to only one a day. I mean, who doesn't like chocolates? This is even better than that!"

Deborah Sharp
Southwest Director
International Messengers

Debbie has so bravely shared her own story of healing and restoration and in doing so reminded us all that our God is more than capable of mending our souls. This is the perfect book for anyone who has ever been made to feel "less than" or "not good enough." If you need to breathe in the fresh air of God's grace today then you need this book!

Christy Fay

Pastor, blogger, and author of

Reclaimed: Uncovering Your Worth

Dedication

I dedicate this book to Jesus, The Master Junker, who reclaimed me from the rag basket of Life's Flea Market. He stitched me up, renewed me, and reused me. One man's trash is Jesus's treasure. I have been "upcycled." Thank you, Jesus, my redeemer, restorer, rebuilder, rewarder.

Acknowledgments

I thank my husband, Tom, who also saved this broken girl more than forty-five years ago. What were you thinking? Your unconditional love and patience healed my broken heart and bound up my wounds, just like Jesus.

Thank you to every Young Life leader (especially Charlie Bowles), "Other Mother," Bible teacher, and "Soul Sister" who poured one vital drop or buckets of Living Water into me. Special thanks to Deborah Sharp and Shela-Lyn Boxberger, who made this book happen.

Table of Contents

Part 3: Vintage Cloth

Preface

Mended: repaired, freed from
faults and defects, improved, put
in working order again.

For the most part, needlework and sewing skills are like VHS tapes and landline phones: gone and almost forgotten. Darning eggs and thimbles—what? But God still does His mending. He gently takes His fragile, worn-out, frayed creations in hand and remakes them again and again. I am one of His mended ones.

Like Gideon, my clan is weak, and I am the least in my father's house. And like Amos, I am a nobody, but "the Lord took me," with no training or aspirations for greatness or leadership, and showed me favor. By His immeasurable grace and patience, He mended my spirit and my life and carried me in His loving arms from "my mother's womb to white hair." My heart's cry is that of King David: Who am I that You have done this for me? And Elizabeth: Why am I so favored? I remain a nobody, a small fish in a small pond, but I have been richly blessed. I never saw it coming, and neither did anyone else. Praise the Lord, for He has dealt bountifully with me!

I have encountered so many women who feel wounded, broken, inadequate, torn, unaccepted, or ashamed and who desperately want to embrace wholeness, freedom, forgiveness, and grace. I have been there, and I am here to assure you that hope is not lost. My message to you is that God can redesign and repurpose anyone at any time for their good and His glory. At the end of each chapter is a suggested affirmation for your own life alterations.

These little thoughts have been gathered from my life, sermon notes, songs, and the inspired words of others jotted in my journals. At the time, I made no mention of authors, nor was I careful with quotations. As a result, I am unable to give credit where credit is due. Not every thought is original to me. However, "every good gift comes from above," and therefore, I will give my Holy "Ghost Writer" the glory.

Introduction

Dear Reader,

My unraveling began at a young age. Like you, perhaps, the small nips and slits of life grew larger over time. Slices and slashes by people and circumstances left me tattered in the rag pile. I was forced to drop out of high school during a teenage pregnancy. Unspeakable pain. However, God was working unseen. He salvaged the scraps of my life and allowed me to become an honored high school Spanish teacher, school board member, wife, and mother. He is the Master Tailor.

The mending has continued for a lifetime. Sometimes people caused the damage. "They are all idiots, and they are all aimed at you," as my father said. "Mirandas" falsely accused me, and "Righteous Brothers" condemned every sin. Ouch! Sometimes circumstances ripped me apart. "Surprise!"

Unwanted, unexpected retirement and social anxiety disorder hacked the fabric of my life. Again and again, Jesus gently patched me with His holy "cross" stitch, through the Word and the Holy Spirit, adding a new hook and eye of purpose and joy.

Be assured, God delights to redesign and repurpose anyone at any time for our good and His glory. Cosmetic surgery for the soul! Find friendship, fellowship, and freedom here; be mended with me. Laugh and eat chocolate with me. Bring your time-worn, stained, fragile, fraying hearts, souls, and lives to Jesus, and be clothed in new garments. No eye has seen, nor ear heard, nor the heart conceived what God has prepared for those who love Him (see 1 Corinthians 2:9).

Damaged
Cloth

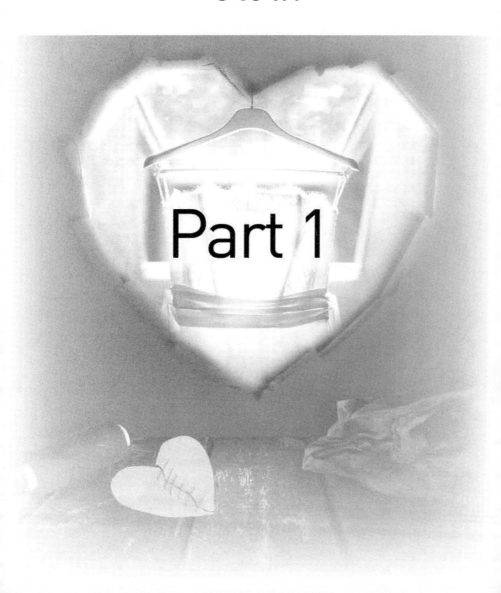

Part 1

CHAPTER 1

Mended (Renewal)

On July 17, I was perfect. God had knit me in my mother's womb, and my frame was not hidden from Him. He beheld my unformed substance and wrote my name in His book. I was fearfully and wonderfully made. He put the Spirit into my bones. He called me by name. He had determined all my days. On July 18, I was born into this fallen world and began to unravel.

Scripture says some will sow and others will reap. I say

some will sew and others will rip! Once I left God's loom, the fraying began. Small nips and snips and slits at first; parents, siblings, neighborhood kids with teasing, taunting, and ignoring. Later came the slices and slashes of teachers, classmates, girlfriends, and boyfriends with mocking, comparing, and betraying. Ouch. Stop it! This Raggedy Ann doll was more raggedy than doll! A few "other-mothers" came to repair me from time to time, patching and redressing me with loving hearts and gentle hands. Still, strangers, even co-workers, came to tear and tug. Cutting remarks and hacking judgments. Smiling Christians pulled out hidden seam rippers to split me wide open. After fifty years of cutting and clipping, I was in tatters, ready for the rag pile.

> # This Raggedy Ann doll was more raggedy than doll!

The apostle Paul certainly had his own rippers and slashers. He lamented to Timothy that "Alexander did me great harm." But he allowed God to deal with Alexander, saying, "The Lord stood by me and gave me strength." And so I would cry, "KB did me great harm!" And I can testify with Paul that "the Lord will rescue me from every evil and save me for His heavenly kingdom" (2 Tim. 4:14–18).

Jesus picked up my shredded scraps. He put me back on His loom and began to mend. "He heals the brokenhearted and binds up their wounds" (Ps. 147:3). "I will restore health to you, and your wounds I will heal" (Jer. 30:17). He rewove me with mercy, love, and compassion. "Thy hands have made and fashioned me" (Ps. 119:73). He knit His Spirit to mine. His Word reinforced me at the torn places. At times, He used a "sewing circle" of precious women to darn peace and joy into my soul.

Still, at times I become fat with pride or swollen with self-pity and burst my seams. Again and again, Jesus comes to repair me. I am no Barbie doll. I am more of a Frankenstein, covered with and mended by stiches, hand-tailored by God. But I am a work of art, a thing of beauty, just as He designed me. My name is still in His book, and I am His special possession (see Malachi 3:16–17).

Today, instead of allowing criticism from other people to hurt me, I will remind myself that God created me in His image, and to Him I am a work of art.

CHAPTER 2

Deborah, "The Bee" (Personal Touch)

Without much thought, my mother named me Deborah. Pretty common in the 1950s, like Cathy, Linda, Susan, and Nancy. And so I became Debbie, like thousands of other Debbies. Didn't like it, didn't hate it, didn't think about it. Didn't know it was a biblical name. Also didn't change the spelling to be unique: "Debi." Never put a heart over the "i." I never even had a

11

nickname or pet name. Not Deb, or Debster, or Debaroo. Just plain, ordinary, nothing unusual, one of thousands, Debbie. Abraham Lincoln said, "God must love the common man, He made so many of them." Right on, Abe!

As a middle child of five siblings, I was nothing special. Much like Gideon, I was the least in my clan (see Judges 6:17). Not a dancer, musician, athlete, genius, artist, or star in any way. I just took up space, living below the radar so as not to bother anyone. My mantra actually became "Don't bother anyone." Stay low, keep quiet, sit in the back. And so it went.

> God directs my working, planning, and organizing.

What I didn't yet realize was that God had surnamed me, though I did not know Him (see Isaiah 45:4). He had called me from my mother's womb and made mention of my name (see Isaiah 49:1). God knew me right well before my birth (see Psalm 139:14). I was Deborah, The Bee, the industrious one. And in truth, I am a bee to my core.

It is well documented that bees are diligent workers

(check), future planners (check), homebodies (check), organized leaders (check), and have discernment (check). They also need time to withdraw from the world and re-energize—check!

How personal and precious to learn that God had intentionally designed me for His good purpose (see Psalm 138:8). Not more than or less than anyone, for God tells us that to compare ourselves with others is foolish (see 2 Corinthians 10:12), but I am unique after all. Go figure!

I am productive for a purpose.

Much of my early life seemed wasted and without purpose. Yet God assures me that there is a time for everything...to weep, laugh, mourn, and dance (see Ecclesiastes 3:1–8). God has restored the years the locusts had eaten (see Joel 2:25). He has made a garland from ashes, giving me the oil of gladness (see Isaiah 61:3).

Yes, bees are common, but they fill a great need in God's creation. Now my buzzing around isn't just busywork. I am productive for a purpose.

God directs my working, planning, and organizing. And after a lifetime, I can rename myself "Deb-bee."

Today, instead of considering myself ordinary and my life without purpose, I will acknowledge the unique and precious gifts God has bestowed on me to glorify His Kingdom.

CHAPTER 3

Straight As (Accepted)

My parents had no interest in me, leaving a hole in my heart and a hunger for straight As: Acceptance. Attention. Approval. Appreciation. They could not or would not be available to me. I tried singing, dancing, playing piano, defeating my brother in challenges, keeping a clean room, being punctual, being seen but not heard, being not seen and not heard. Still no affirmation, no confirmation. I tried and kept on trying because an unconnected life is not worth living. I would look elsewhere.

Straight As: Acceptance. Attention. Approval. Appreciation. Maybe school, teachers, and classmates could fill the hole. I had a new audience. Give 'em the old razzle-dazzle, right? Years of high grades, honor societies, leadership positions, athletic successes, homecoming queen nominations, and finally graduation from the university magna cum laude with straight As. Acceptance. Attention. Approval. Appreciation. But not for long.

Grown-up, real life does not offer report cards. What's up with that? How will I earn my straight As? Where will I find validation? How will I fill this hole in my heart? Who will give me the acceptance and approval I crave?

Jesus. Only Jesus. God, the Creator of all things, has chosen me, by His grace, and made me *acceptable* in the Beloved (see Ephesians 1:3–6). Therefore, I am free from the tyranny of public opinion! I can live a quiet and peaceable life, with godliness and reverence, and be *acceptable* in the sight of God (see 1 Timothy 2:3). Therefore, I am free from good works and feats of strength! When I serve Jesus with righteousness, peace, and joy in the Holy Spirit, I am *acceptable* and *approved* by God Himself (see Romans

14:18). Therefore, I am free from the bondage of human approval! When I rightly divide the Word of God, I am *approved* by the God of the Universe (see 2 Timothy 2:15). When I am grateful and reverent, I am *acceptable* to the One True God (see Hebrews 12:28). There is nothing I can do to make God love me more, and there is nothing I can do to make God love me less. For freedom, Jesus has set me free (see Galatians 5:1). Free from the crushing burden of proving myself to society, family, other people, and even to myself. I am no longer enslaved to a report card.

If God is for me, who can be against me (see Romans 8:31)? Not Mother or Father, friend or stranger, angels or principalities. If I

Grown-up, real life does not offer report cards.

am still striving to please men, I am not a servant of Christ (see Galatians 1:10). This I know, that God is for me. What can man do to me (see Psalm 56:10–11)? Not one drop of my worth depends on the acceptance, attention, approval, or appreciation of others. I no longer let others define me. I no longer need straight As. My heart has been filled by the grace of God, and I am *acceptable* in the Beloved. I, like the disciple John, am the one Jesus loves (see John 2:19).

Today I will stop striving to win the acceptance, attention, approval, or appreciation of other people and bask in the contentment of knowing that God loves and accepts me already.

CHAPTER 4

Meanwhile, God...
(God Works Unseen)

When Jacob saw Joseph's bloody coat of many colors, he cried that without a doubt, his precious son had been ripped to pieces. He tore his own clothes, put on sackcloth, mourned, and refused to be comforted. But, as always, all the *known* facts are not *all* the facts. *Meanwhile*, God was working in Egypt (See Genesis 37:36). Joseph had actually been sold to Potiphar. The Lord was with him, showed him mercy, and gave him favor. It was God's perfect plan to humble and mature Joseph and later save Israel, fulfilling God's promise to Abraham. Years later, when Jacob and Joseph were reunited, Jacob glorified God, saying, "I had not thought to see your face; but in fact God has also shown me your sons!" (see Genesis 37, 39, 45, and 48.)

References in Scripture to the phrase "*Meanwhile, God...*" remind us that while we are living our daily lives, God is orchestrating something magnificent in the background.

As Moses and the children of Israel fled, the Egyptians pursued them, and the Israelites were terrified. The people were caught between the waters before them and Pharaoh's army behind them. But again, all the known facts were not all the facts. *Meanwhile*, God was working unseen all that night (see Exodus 14:19–23). He hid Israel with a cloud of darkness, parted the waters for safe crossing, confused the Egyptians, and delivered the people safely. "When they saw this great work they feared and believed the Lord" (Ex. 14:31).

My family home was not a place of nurturing. There was barely supervision. I fumbled along, following others, finding my way. I ached for attention and guidance. *Meanwhile*, God was working in Egypt. Other-Mothers were being prepared and sent to foster me. "Adopted" soul sisters came along to safeguard me. And Young Life leaders were being equipped to direct me to Jesus. The Lord was with me, like Joseph, showing great mercy and giving me favor. Precious, unseen mending.

> **I am confident that God is working unseen.**

Exodus 14:22 says, "So the people of Israel walked through the middle of the sea on dry ground, with walls of water on each side!" God shielded the Israelites from the danger that surrounded them. He did the same for me. The unspeakable pain of a teenage pregnancy and the adoption of my unseen, unnamed baby left me confused, hopeless, and suicidal. *Meanwhile*, God was working unseen. By His grace and divine intervention, He protected me from enemies behind and the terrifying waters ahead. He shielded me as I walked through the middle of the "sea" on dry ground and allowed me to meet my husband and graduate with high honors from the university I attended. Both were unimaginable victories—miracles, really. Then later, to be blessed with three sons? That was just God showing off! And tenderly mending.

Humble and rejoicing, I sing to the Lord as David did. "Who am I, O Lord, that You have brought me this far? And yet it is a small thing in Your sight . . . For Your Word's sake, and according to Your own heart, You have done all these great things to make your servant know them. You are great, O Lord, and there is none besides You" (see 2 Samuel 7:18).

As life unfolds—whether through illness, aging parents, the challenge of a prodigal son, or tragedy—I am certain that all the known facts are not all the facts. I am confident that God is working unseen. This I know, that God is for me (see Psalm 56:9), and I shall see the goodness of the Lord in the land of the living (see Psalm 27:13). I am assured that His purposes are for my good and His glory. His plans for me will not be thwarted (see Job 42:2).

Today I will stop focusing on the aspects of my life that are not ideal and realize that God is working, meanwhile, in the background to make miracles happen.

CHAPTER 5

The Righteous Brothers
(Forgiveness and Freedom)

An older Christian woman, "Mrs. Righteous," boldly proclaimed to anyone who would listen that she had not sinned (ever) since the day she was saved by Jesus Christ. She was a real peach! I had no dealings with her personally, but I did meet her sons, R. Righteous and D. Righteous. Legalistic and perfect themselves, they had not fallen far from the "Peach Tree."

As a new babe in Christ, lost and profoundly damaged by sin and its severe consequences, I lived my life at the university trying to redeem myself: no drinking, no drugs, perfect class attendance, straight As. I was also attending a Bible study, where I met the Righteous Brothers. My safe place of unconditional love and forgiveness was quietly poisoned with judgment and condemnation.

Stupidly, I became a smoker in college. Not much; maybe a pack a week. Just something cool to do, right, like everyone else. Holy moly! This was intolerable to R. Righteous. Unthinkable. He was eager to tell me that I couldn't have a Christian testimony if I smoked. I may not have been saved at all! I had to quit smoking, according to the gospel of R. Righteous.

Oh, precious Holy Spirit, newly flickering in me. In my confusion over the harsh criticism, I could hear the Holy Spirit whispering, "Never mind him; don't believe that. We will get to the smoking later. You have *many* more serious issues than that! You are a mess, you are forgiven, and you are loved. There is nothing more to do. Let Me heal you." I did not know then, but learned later, how the Holy Spirit intercedes for us with sighs too deep for words, according to the will of God (see Romans 8:26–27). And mends.

I wore holy earplugs when the Righteous Brothers were around. Satan was prowling like a lion, looking to devour me, a new lamb in the faith. The enemy did not want another soul testifying to the glory of God! But The Good Shepherd would not allow it. Jesus Christ the Righteous is the atonement for my sin (see John 2:2). If I confess my sin, He is faithful to forgive me and cleanse me from all unrighteousness (see John 1:9). Having received the Spirit by grace, it is foolish to return to works of the flesh (see Galatians 3:3). Yay! For freedom, Christ has set me free. I will not return to the yoke of slavery (see Galatians 5:1). There is nothing to earn and nothing to prove. More yay!

> Satan was prowling like a lion, looking to devour me, a new lamb in the faith.

I also came to understand that believers should have no self-conceit and should not provoke one another. We are to restore one another in a spirit of gentleness (see Galatians 5:26, 6:1). I have encountered other Righteous Brothers through the years, but I recognize and dismiss them now. If pressed, I say with a confident smile, "Yes, I sin differently than you." That ends the conversation, for sure.

As for Mr. R. Righteous, he never smoked. Yet after thirty-plus years of marriage to a precious, long-suffering saint, he was revealed to be a serial adulterer and a deeply-in-debt online gambler, among other things. I took no pleasure in his fall. He just sins differently than me. Saddened by the damaged lives he left in his wake, I thank God I was not one of his victims. The patchwork of redemption and renewal Jesus stitched on my heart has held tight.

Today I will ignore the judgments others make about me and claim God's forgiveness, mercy, and grace.

CHAPTER 6

Lazarus and Me (The Victory, Not the War)

Some women love to retell their harrowing stories of labor and childbirth. It is almost a competition. Whose was longer, harder, most horrific? To add authority and finality, they add comments by medical personnel: "My doctor said it was the worst labor he had ever attended!" "The nurse said she had never seen anything more dreadful." Agonizing! Tortured! Near fatal! I learned to hold my tongue; there was no point. But just for the record, my first labor and delivery lasted fifteen hours. I was alone in my room (no parents, no husband, no breathing coach) with no pain medication, and then naked on a cold X-ray table, and finally, ripped stem to stern and ending with a breech birth. Just sayin'. I needed serious mending. Stitches, anyone?

Some Christians love to retell their life story before Jesus. Whose was more abused, neglected, sad, tragic, and heartbreaking? Or whose was more sinful, wicked, shameful, and scandalous? Although I didn't often speak of my back story, in my heart I focused more on the "before" than the "after." I allowed questions, sorrow, and self-pity to dominate my narrative.

Then I met Lazarus (see John 11). I imagined his back story: "I loved Jesus; I was his friend. My sisters and I served him faithfully. We were braver and more devoted than anyone. We were part of His inner circle. Then I got sick. You can't imagine how I suffered. My doctor said he had never seen a more agonizing case! My sisters were devastated. When the doctor said it would be fatal, we sent for Jesus, but He didn't even bother to come! Can you believe it? After all we did for Him? Well, He came later and resurrected me, but have you ever heard of such unnecessary suffering? I wouldn't wish that on my worst enemy."

But Jesus had withheld his blessing to increase it. He did not hurry to restore Lazarus and relieve his sisters' sorrow. He waited for the glory of God. He had his eye on the eternal spectrum, not on their personal comfort. Jesus called Lazarus out of the grave by name so that others might believe in the One who had sent him.

And so it is with me. Jesus waited as I was dead in sin. But in the fullness of time, He commanded others to roll the stone away, removing the obstacle between us, and called me by name out of death and into life. He commanded others to unbind me from my grave clothes and teach me to walk by faith. Jesus set me at liberty to testify to the miracle and His glory.

> # Lazarus did not tarry or go back to his putrid bindings, and neither should I.

Lazarus did not tarry or go back to his putrid bindings, and neither should I. The grave of this world is no place for those whom Christ has quickened (see Ephesians 2). We must come forth, laying aside every hindrance. Satan calls me back to focus on old pain, injustice, and unkindness to distract from the mercy and grace of Jesus, saying, "Look at those old bindings and smell them again. Remember what you went through?" No, God gives us the oil of gladness instead of mourning and a garment of praise instead of a spirit of despair (see Isaiah 61:3). He has rewoven me and put me in working order again. Instead, I will remember my new song: "What a Friend We Have in Jesus."

Today I will leave my mistakes, disappointments, worries, and despair behind and let gratitude flow through my heart for all of the ways I am blessed.

Savaged
Cloth

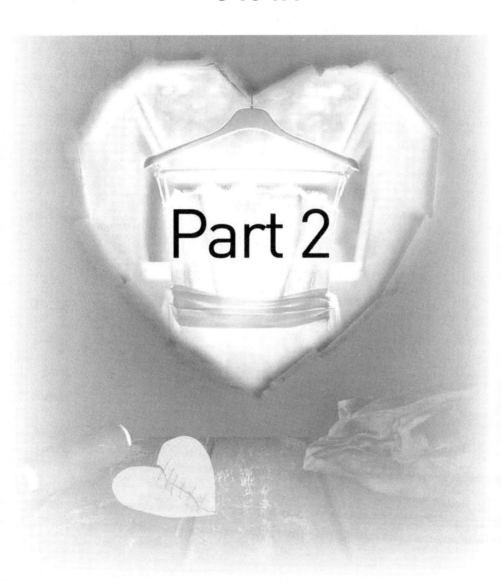

Part 2

CHAPTER 7

Happy Camper (Joy)

I am not a happy camper. By nature, my temperament is melancholy, sad. By nurture, I am cynical, glass half-empty. I once read a greeting card that said, "I'm comfortable with the fact that my glass will always have a slow and steady leak." Amen!

My husband is by nature sanguine, cheerful. Even more so by nurture. His mother was the happiest place on earth. Disneyland had nothing on her. She pulled me outside by my arm one night to come see a "fun moon." Really. "Fun" was her middle name, and my hubby is her clone. When he wakes up, he greets me with his big, beautiful smile, saying, "Hi, lover!" When I wake up, my first thought is, "Oh, crap. I'm still here." Oh, yeah. "This is the day the Lord has made. I *will* rejoice and be glad in it" (Ps. 118:24, emphasis added).

> When old feelings return, I can stand on faith and trust His Word.

A dear friend can relate. She told me, "Some of us are just Eeyores, and no amount of encouragement from Tigger can change us." Love that. Give it a rest, Tigger.

I need a Super Hero, and I have one. Gratefully, my nature has been overcome by my "supernatural" God. My old nature, my old self, is dead, and I am alive in Christ (see Romans 6:6, Galatians 2:20). I am not enslaved to my old mind-set. Jesus graciously transforms my mind. I am sealed with the Holy Spirit and can develop His fruit of joy (see Ephesians 1:13 and Galatians 5:22). This is an unknown, exotic fruit to me. Like rambutan, ackee, physalis, and durian. What is this?

In truth, my fallen personality is gone. I need not strive to overcome. When old feelings return, I can stand on faith and trust His Word. No matter what I see in the natural or physical realm, truth stands. I go to God's Word. "Thy words were found and I ate them, and thy words became to me the joy and delight of my heart" (Jer. 15:16). I take my feelings to the cross. Martin Luther said we must fight like hell for joy. Habakkuk 3:18 says, "I will joy in the God of my salvation." I will; it is my will; I will fight for joy! At times it is just my will, but later my heart and emotions follow. Although I may not always feel joy, I can be thankful in all things. And joy can be found at the table of thanksgiving. I will cultivate a thankful heart.

> # I am learning. Only self can kill joy.

I am learning. Only self can kill joy. Helen Keller said, "There is joy in self-forgetfulness." By grace, I set my mind on the Spirit, which is life and peace (see Romans 8:6). Fruit, anyone? Love, joy, peace, patience . . . ?

For me, joy is a process. Refusing to be cheerless, I plug

my leaky, half-filled glass daily and let God fill me to the brim. "My cup overflows!" (Ps. 23:5). I may never be my mother-in-law, but God gets the glory when I find joy. It is a stunning transformation only He can make.

Today, if I find myself beginning to complain or grumble, I will consciously replace my negativity with joy and cheerfulness.

CHAPTER 8

My Father vs. *THE* Father (Grace)

They are all idiots, and they are all aimed at you!" Words of wisdom from my father as he taught me to drive. Look out—expect the unexpected from the fools around you. "They are all idiots and all aimed at you" became a life motto for me. At the mall, at the grocery store, at the theater, in the school car pool pickup lane, in the church parking lot. "We hold these truths to be self-evident." I saw a piece of unframed art in an interior design store. Adorable 1950s child with a hair bow, a rose in her hand, and a blank stare. Next to her is the dictionary definition of "idiot": mentally defective, imbecile, moron, fool, witling. Below, in large graphic print, is the caption "Most of the people around me on any given day." Can I get an Amen?

> Should I honk or just run them off the road to teach them a lesson?

But then I met THE Father. And Amy Grant sang of "My Father's Eyes." And Jesus saw me as a child who had not been loved enough. And Jesus looked beyond my faults and saw my needs. And Jesus had compassion on me, helpless and harassed like a sheep without a shepherd (see Matthew 9:36). And I was awed that Jesus walked among the crowds and masses of people, the idiots, fools, and morons, with love and without irritation. And I was humbled by grace. And THE Father gave me grace-colored glasses to see others as my companions in woundedness. And THE Father instructed me to accept life (and people) with humility and patience, making allowances for them" (see Ephesians 4:2, Colossians 3:12). And THE

Father filled me with his Spirit and the fruit of love, peace, patience, and gentleness (see Galatians 5:22).

I now wear prescription bifocal sunglasses to drive. This requires me to remove my grace-colored glasses. Now I'm in traffic with my father's voice in my head again. "They are all idiots, and they are all aimed at you!" Heaven help me! I know, Daddy, I know. Should I honk or just run them off the road to teach them a lesson? Maybe they are just normal people in their normal confusion on a normal day, like me. Maybe I should make peace with flawed humanity. Maybe I should make allowances for them, as Jesus does for me. Maybe they, too, are slashed and shredded, in need of mending. Can I get an Amen?

Today, if I catch myself finding fault with someone, I will look beyond their faults and show compassion for their needs, just as Jesus does for me every day. Today I will practice exhibiting patience, humility, and kindness, not just to the people I care about but to strangers as well.

CHAPTER 9

More Idiots (Compassion)

Yes, Daddy, I remember they are all idiots, and they are all aimed at me. I know that now, not because you warned me, but because it is my life experience. In the baseball bleachers. At the antique show. In the library. At the nail salon. Everywhere. Idiots.

But you were right about drivers, Daddy. Drivers are the worst. One day, as I waited behind others in a left-hand turn lane, I grew impatient. If I didn't make this light, my son would be late for preschool. Tragic. Unforgivable. Several opportunities to turn went by with no one moving. Grrrr . . . Finally, the light turned red, and the first car turned. Bam! The slow, patient idiot was hit broadside by a *bigger* idiot running the light! Now we will be late no matter what. I needed to stay as a witness so the bigger idiot was known to police. Thankfully, no one was seriously hurt. My life continued to be filled with idiots.

Why give grace to a friend, but not a stranger?

Weeks later, a similar left-turn situation arose, but I was not as far back in line. Surely I would make this one. But nooo . . . Another space cadet not paying attention and not turning when there was a chance. Hey, moron, you are not the only one who wants to turn today. Move it! When she finally did turn, I recognized her as a friend and had to laugh. Oh, of course it's her. She's clueless, but I love her. No problem. My irritation vanished. I did not make the light, but I was no longer angry. I gave her grace.

Wait a minute, there. Why give grace to a friend, but not a stranger? Jesus said, "As you wish men would do unto you, do so unto them. Even sinners love those who love them. And if you do good to those who do good unto you, what credit is that to you? Love your enemies, and do good. Be merciful, even as your Father is merciful unto you" (see Luke 6:32–36).

I'm in trouble. Love the idiots and show mercy? Not just to those I know and love and understand and care about, but show compassion and sympathy to the idiots, too? Really? Yes, you hypocrite, take the log out of your own eye first (see Luke 6:42). You, too, are an idiot on any given day. Just ask your friends and family!

Forgive me, Father. I lack humility and patience. Mend my preprogrammed thoughts. Sew your kindness and gentleness to my spirit. I do not make allowances for others (see Ephesians 4:2, Colossians 3:12–13). I judge harshly, not giving the benefit of the doubt. I do not know the sorrow, pain, and stress others bear. Before criticizing others, I need to have an "I" examination. I am an idiot.

Today I will practice exhibiting patience, humility, and kindness, not just to the people I care about but to strangers as well.

CHAPTER 10

White Rabbit (God's Agenda)

Tickticktickticktick. I have a constant, subconscious clock ticking in my head. Always. At times it is helpful. At times it is torture. Do you hear it? Tickticktickticktick. I am the White Rabbit from Alice in Wonderland. "I'm late, I'm late, for a very important date!" Always. Yet no one else seems to sense the urgency or the importance of my distress. Come on, people! Get with it!

Perhaps it is genetic. My father and his father both worked

as efficiency experts for a time at the Goodyear Tire & Rubber factory in Ohio. Don't work harder; work smarter. Plan ahead. Understand the big picture. See all the moving parts. Do it faster and better. No excuses. Get 'er done! When my father died, I inherited his father's stopwatch from his factory days. I also inherited his and his father's inner clock.

Both by nature and by nurture, I became The White Rabbit.

My mother quietly reinforced a life of schedules and efficiency. As a working mom with five children, she ran our home with the order of an Army camp. Her day began at 5:00 a.m. to dress, clean house or do a load of laundry, and fix breakfast for her family of seven. ("Back in the day," there were no microwaves or premade meals. No Egg McMuffins.) She woke the rest of us at 6:00 to dress, eat, and be out the door by 7:30. Mother was a domestic efficiency engineer. No rushing, no panic, no missing shoes or coats, no lost homework. Planned. Organized. Routine. Tickticktick.

Both by nature and by nurture, I became The White

46

Rabbit. My life was well ordered. A place for everything and everything in its place. Until a husband and three sons came along. I fell down the Rabbit Hole, and life became curiouser and curiouser.

No problem. The Proverbs 31 woman "looks well to the ways of her household. She works with willing hands. She rises while it is still night and provides food for her household (just like my mom). Her lamp does not go out at night. She does not eat the bread of idleness" (Prov. 31:27). Order and harmony were possible. After all, Jesus ordered the five thousand into small groups before feeding them (see Mark 6:39). What efficiency! And God did not create the world in chaos, but order, for our well-being (see Isaiah 48:18 and 1 Corinthians 14:33). Systematic, regulated, methodized. Heaven on earth.

No problem. Create a personal calendar, add a master family calendar, and get started. Look ahead; plan ahead; work ahead. My mind was always three hours ahead, three days ahead, three months ahead. I didn't have a life; I had a schedule. "Hey," I warned, "watch out, or off with your head!" I didn't have joy in the present, and I rarely found joy in His Presence.

Problem: pressure and stress agitated and vexed me.

Even chocolate wasn't working. No Fruit of the Spirit (peace, patience) grew on my tree. I was attentive and watchful, even hypervigilant, to anticipate every need, every event, every holiday. The ticking did not stop until I looked to Jesus.

When Jesus walked on earth, He had no blueprint or preplanned schedule. He discerned the Father's will day by day in a life of prayer. He walked through each day decisively and without irritation, knowing what needed to be done.

> I want to accept the gift of each day.

"Give us this day our *daily* bread." I want to be a day-to-day person. I want to accept the gift of each day. God is a lamp unto my feet, showing me each next step (see Psalm 119:105), as opposed to a beacon or a floodlight, showing me the next five miles. Relying on God has to begin again each day.

My White Rabbit is not yet completely contained, but he is on a leash. I still hear a faint tickticktick. But God's Word assures me that in the night, the Lord instructs my heart (see Psalm 16:17). I shall hear a word saying, "This is the way; walk in it" (see Isaiah 30:21). A woman may plan her way, but God directs her steps (see Proverbs 16:9). Now, my "very important date" is with the Lord, before I fill up my calendar.

Today I will release the pressure I put on myself to have everything in perfect order and realize that I am not in control—God is.

CHAPTER 11

Do vs. Done
(Called, Not Driven)

I t is finished" (John 19:30). Christ assured us from the cross that there was nothing more to be done. This is the glorious, victorious difference between Christianity and all other religions. We do not need Christ plus church attendance, Christ plus baptism, or Christ plus fasting. Not Christ plus good deeds or good behavior. We are saved by Christ plus nothing. It is finished!

I believed this Gospel doctrine and then joyfully entered into faith that was active along with works (see James 2:22–26). Adult Ministries (missions, hospitality, event coordinator) volunteer, Bible Study leader, hostess for studies in my home, leader for Mexico mission trips, Proverbs 31 woman personified. It took a while for me to learn to be called, not driven. "There is a time for every matter under heaven" (Eccles. 3:1).

God determined the time for that lesson in my life. I never saw it coming. God moved me unexpectedly to a desert place, to speak tenderly to me. He would give me hope, and I would return to Him, as in the days of my youth (see Hosea 2:14). The next year I left my job, again unforeseen. And then my world turned upside down. Gripped by social anxiety disorder (SAD, ironically), everything was canceled, even the precious Bible study I led. I couldn't explain why.

I had been in God's Waiting Room before. Eventually the Great Physician would see me, heal me, and send me on my way. I was prepared to wait again. But this was to be a very distinctive appointment: ten years in the Waiting Room. Time to learn the difference between do and done.

I saw no one, went almost nowhere. Getting groceries was a nightmare. Answering the phone gave me heart palpitations. I struggled to pray, forced myself to read the Bible, and sang hymns in desperation. Humbled and embarrassed not to be "doing," I fought on, concerned about how little I cared. Frustrated, there was nothing I could "do" about it. Eventually I didn't care that I didn't care! I was a dry desert, a barren wasteland. This was my new normal, and I was OK with it. But God was working unseen, in my dark place, as always, for my good and His glory (see Exodus 14:19–22).

> # I was a dry desert, a barren wasteland.

When I could not and would not *do*, I learned it was already *done*. It is finished; God is doing the work now. Nothing I can *do* will make Him love me more; nothing I can *do* would make Him love me less. Jesus is interceding for me at the right hand of the Father. The Holy Spirit is pleading for me. The Father Himself is singing over me. "I am doing a new thing . . . I will make a way in the wilderness and rivers in the desert . . . that my people I formed for myself shall declare my praise" (see Isaiah 43:18–21).

Others have been found and saved in the desert. Hagar (see Genesis 21), Moses (see Exodus 3, 4), John the Baptist (see Luke 3) and even Jesus (see Luke 4) encountered God in the wilderness. Destiny is found in the desert. It is a place of wondering, wandering, and questioning, a place of struggle. But it's the place where God shows up. "I will make her wilderness like a garden. Joy and thanksgiving will be found in her" (Isa. 51:3). Jesus can heal the brokenhearted and bind up wounds in the desert.

God indeed, literally, moved me to a desert place. We still live there. But as promised, He has done great things for me (see Psalm 126:3). He has filled my mouth with laughter and my tongue with shouts of joy. Jesus spent ten years darning and patching me with His gentle hands. I am His renewed creation.

I still have a "to do" list. But now I am a sheep who listens for the voice of my Good Shepherd. He calls me by name and leads me (see John 10:3). I listen, like Elijah, for the still, small voice of God (see 1 Kings 19:12). "Your ears shall hear a word behind you saying, "This is the way; walk in it" (Isa. 30:21). Stand in the road and ask where the good path is; walk in it and find rest for your souls (see Jeremiah 6:16). Everything else is done.

Today I will release myself from the burden of feeling like I always have to do something. I will derive peace from the realization that Jesus has done the most important act of all—dying for our sins on the cross.

CHAPTER 12

Little Santas (Priorities)

December. The boys were at school, and I spent the entire day decorating for Christmas. Daily decor removed, anything Christmas in its place. Red and green candles everywhere. Red and green cushions for the kitchen chairs, red and green towels in the bathrooms and kitchen. Christmas bath mats, doormats, and throw rugs. Snowflake-snowman Kleenex box covers. Christmas Spode dishes and decor pieces. Ornaments hung from the kitchen pot rack and chandelier. A vast nutcracker display. Wreaths. Reindeer. A hand-carved Nativity scene in the family room and a Hummel Nativity scene in the living room. On and on, hour after hour. No flat surface went unadorned. Even the inside of a large antique display cabinet with glass doors was filled. But my favorite was my Santa collection. All shapes, all sizes. Wood, china, porcelain, fabric, glass. Adorable, elegant, traditional, contemporary, vintage. Everywhere.

The Holy Spirit was quick to convict me.

Exhausted, yet exhilarated, I picked up the boys after school. Beaming with delight and anticipation, I led them into our Christmas wonderland. My middle son, just a first-grader, was known to be blunt, bold, and direct. After barely a glance, he proclaimed, "Too much Santa; not enough Jesus" and walked casually to his room. Pierced to the core, my soul ached. He was right, of course, but I didn't want to hear it. But look how cute, how beautiful, how fun. Look! Look! We have Jesus every day, but can't we just have some Santa, too?

The Holy Spirit was quick to convict me. The Santas were donated. I think of them fondly at Christmas, with a smile and a precious memory. But God didn't let it end there.

What else do I have too much of that crowds out Jesus? What is dimming my light and overshadowing Jesus (see Matthew 5:14–16)? The Beatitudes teach the qualities God wants to develop in me (see Matthew 5:3–12). How am I doing?

- Too much wardrobe, not enough humility?

- Too much makeup, not enough repentance?

- Too much television, not enough obedience?

- Too much chocolate, not enough spiritual hunger?

- Too much judging, not enough mercy?

- Too much jewelry, not enough purity?

- Too much exercise, not enough peace making?

- Too much self-justifying, not enough righteousness?

Too much me, not enough Jesus! Ouch! Time to get rid of more stuff, more distractions, and get back to Jesus. It takes a long time. Some little "Santas" are hard to give up. It is exhausting work, but exhilarating.

Today I will identify the things in my life that distract me from Jesus and vow to give them less prominence.

CHAPTER 13

Special Needs (Kindness)

By God's design and to my surprise, I have become deeply involved with a delightful young family. The first son and his twin brothers are only twenty months apart in age. Quite a challenge for any mom right there. But in addition, the eldest has autism, and the twins have craniosynostosis, a genetic disorder that affects the skull, neck, head, face, mouth, teeth, and hands. Multiple surgeries and complicated orthodontia are required, along with various ongoing physical and speech therapies. Later their sister was born. She, too, has developmental needs. Each child is a delight with unique talents, gifts, and personalities. They enrich my life.

I have spent thousands of hours with these kids, frequently out in public for an adventure together. Generally, I'm too busy directing and supervising them to notice those around us. But over the years, I've drawn a conclusion regarding people observing us. When the children with an unusual appearance act inappropriately, I see sympathetic smiles and nods. Some people will comment on my patience or kindness in the situation. But when the child who appears normal is behaving oddly, I see critical looks and disdain. I believe the assumption is that the child isn't well trained or disciplined, in need of correction. No mercy or compassion is offered.

I was shopping at Target one day as a mom walked toward me with her cart. Her daughter was a short distance behind, walking in a silly way, bobbing her head, and loudly saying something I could not understand. She seemed joyful, so I smiled. As I passed them, the mom stopped abruptly and touched my arm. With tears in her eyes, she said, "Thank you for smiling. Most people give us dirty looks. My daughter is having a difficult day." My heart broke as she hugged me, a total stranger in the middle of Target, for one simple smile. It made her day. Like a gift of chocolate.

It occurs to me that we are all special-needs people. We are all fighting a battle, whether seen or unseen. We are all wounded, whether the scars are obvious or not. Dressed in our Sunday best, the tragedy, abuse, violence, pain, neglect, injustices, mental illness, physical illness, and spiritual torment of our lives are neatly tucked in and covered up. Add a smile, and "we clean up real good." Others assume we are well balanced, well trained, and well prepared to be well behaved in any situation. If we aren't, criticism and disapproval abound. If our "disorders" and "developmental needs" were known, perhaps others would respond with compassion instead of judgment. Maybe they would respond with "chocolate."

> There are stitches, scars, and braces holding us all together.

As God, The Great Physician, tends to each of us, let us remember to show grace, kindness, and gentleness to His other patients. "Be kind to one another, tenderhearted, forgiving one another, as God in Christ forgave you" (Eph. 4:32). "In humility, count others better than yourselves" (Phil. 2:3). Do not be fooled by the Sunday Best; there are stitches, scars, and braces holding us all together beneath the coverings. We are a brotherhood of The Mended. "Have unity of spirit, sympathy, love of the brethren, a tender heart, and a humble mind" (1 Peter 3:8).

Today I will recognize that we all have special needs, even if they are not visible, and that God, the Great Physician, is the only One Who can meet those needs.

CHAPTER 14

I Am Not a Snapshot (Judgment)

If I observe someone for a moment on any given day, I may take a mental snapshot that becomes a snap judgment. Maybe it is positive; maybe it is negative. It is never the entire picture. I need a longer video and a personal interview to determine who they really are.

In high school, I was a quiet follower. My friends tried

out for the cheer line, so I did, too. To my surprise, I made the squad, but I was never comfortable in front of crowds. In biology class, we were assigned lab partners. After two days with mine, she confessed to me that she didn't want to be with me at first because I was a cheerleader. She thought I was stuck-up, mean, or stupid. She was happy to discover that I was smart and kind. We got As together in biology, and she was eager to see me again at our twenty-five-year school reunion. I am not a snapshot.

During many years of debilitating PMS, I struggled with everything, especially motherhood. Brain fog, chocolate cravings, hypersensitive hearing, depression, rage. I was a lunatic. Before I could receive medication and treatment, I was required to see a psychologist. After discussing my youth (unfortunate), my marriage (wonderful), and my drug or alcohol usage (none), the doctor concluded that I "was amazingly well adjusted for all I had been through." It actually was hormonal, not a personality disorder, as I had been saying all along. No need for therapy, just medical help. And chocolate. I am not a snapshot.

I was a young mother and lowly substitute teacher when the school board president invited me to join the board. He was a man I did not know. Who, me? I had not sought, asked, hinted, manipulated, politicked, or applied for the position. OK, Lord, but this seems crazy. As a woman on a male-dominated school board, I was required to be assertive and outspoken just to be acknowledged. Not my nature; I'm a "head down, sit in the back" girl. Coming from a female family and working in a female profession did not prepare me for this. I began to read articles on how to survive in a male culture, determined to contribute the skills and gifts God had given me. A male colleague opined that it must be difficult for my husband to live with me. Stunned and hurt, I was quick to inform him that my

> My board "persona" was what God needed me to be in that unique setting.

husband was the head of our home, and I was quite happy to submit to his leadership. He was extremely proud of my contribution, coaching me on how to respond to dismissive, disrespectful men. My board "persona" was what God needed me to be in that unique setting. I am not a snapshot.

While I enjoy jewelry, fashion, and manicures, I also go on mission trips with high school students to Mexico. Some have commented that they cannot imagine me there. Days of hard manual labor, hot temperatures, dirty clothes, a few cold showers, gang toilets, sleeping bags on concrete slabs in open-air shelters, boiling our own water, and cooking our own food. Barely the basics, but I continued to go. I am not a snapshot.

One moment, one day, one social setting may result in one snapshot. But life requires a video camera. One day Paul was a coat rack at Stephen's martyrdom; later he preached Jesus to the world. One day Peter was an uneducated fisherman; another day he denied Christ three times; later he led the early church.

People are complicated. Life is complicated. I must not take snapshots. Or snap judgments, either. "Do not judge by appearances, but judge with right judgment" (John 7:24). I may take videos, but I must leave them for the one Just and Righteous Judge, who sees the entire picture (2 Tim. 4:1, 8).

Today I will avoid making judgments about people based on what I see, and I will acknowledge that each of us is much more than what appears on the surface.

CHAPTER 15

Is Your Middle Name Miranda? (Critical Spirit)

In any group of women, there will always be at least one Miranda. You may not know which one she is because Miranda is her middle name. But she is always there, speaking to you silently: "You have the right to remain silent. Anything you say can and will be held against you." She is judging, criticizing, misinterpreting, and condemning every word you speak. She can and will hold it against you.

She will not confront you personally or privately, or seek understanding, but she will happily tell others. No chance to defend or explain yourself. No benefit of the doubt. You are guilty!

Miss Miranda loves to say, "She acts like she's perfect." "She thinks she's so smart." "She thinks her children are perfect." "She acts like she's better than everyone." "She thinks—."

You have met her, haven't you? Or maybe you *are* her. Is Miranda *your* middle name?

Paul warned Timothy about women who become idlers, gossips, and busybodies, full of worthless talk and harmful, divisive words, "saying what they should not" (see 1 Timothy 5:13). He says gullible, weak women can be taken captive like prisoners of war in the spiritual battle for their hearts and minds. Arrogant slanderers and empty religious people make their way into homes to fool and destroy. He warns, "Avoid such people" (2 Tim. 3:5). Paul had his own Mirandas (see Acts 13:49–52). After he spoke in Antioch, the Gentiles heard and were glad and glorified the Word of God. But others incited the devout women of prominence and high standing— the Mirandas—to stir up persecution and drive Paul and

Barnabas from the city. But Paul shook the dust off his feet against them, filled with joy and the Holy Spirit. These same Mirandas cause tearing, slitting, and division in the body of Christ today. They keep the Great Tailor busy mending.

Jesus said, "Out of the abundance of the heart the mouth speaks" (Matt. 12:34). What Miranda says reveals her own heart. The good woman out of her good treasure brings forth good, and the evil woman out of her evil treasure brings forth evil. Hurting people hurt people. Every woman will be held accountable for every careless word she utters, for by our words we will be justified or condemned on Judgment Day. What does your mouth reveal about you? I confess that I, too, have been Miranda, to my regret and shame. Forgive me, Jesus, and sew up those I have ripped open.

> A woman's heart and motives clarify her actions.

Kelly Clarkson powerfully sings, "You don't know a thing about me." A woman's heart and motives clarify her actions. Each of us has known the sting of misjudgment. Shake the dust off your feet, and be filled with the Holy Spirit. Miranda must seek the truth and understanding before forming and spreading her opinions. If she doesn't, then avoid such people. And if it is you, it's not too late to change your middle name.

Today I vow to stop passing judgment on others and participating in gossip.

Vintage
Cloth

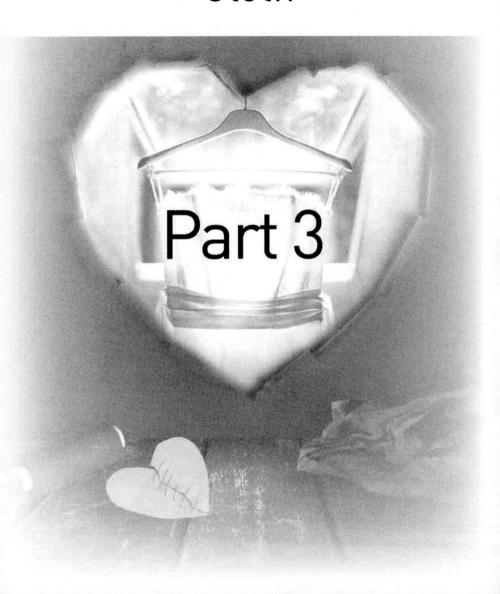

Part 3

CHAPTER 16

Premature Aging
(Wrinkled, Not Obsolete)

God graciously and delightfully answered my prayer for a female roommate. Teaching Spanish part time required that I share a classroom with other teachers. My roommates were various male coaches who also needed a classroom just a few hours each day. While I loved my colorful, creative, neat, and orderly room, it was lost on the men. They had no appreciation or respect for "my" space. Items were moved, lost, borrowed, stolen, broken, or ruined daily. My heart skipped a beat when I learned my new roomie would be a female, but also a total stranger. Praise the Lord, she was fun, creative, tidy, organized, and, as one of ten children, accustomed to sharing! She also kept chocolate in her desk drawer.

We clicked from Day One. So smooth, so easy, like Soul Sisters. Oh, happy day! But after a week or two, she spoke the heart-piercing words, "My friends and I are looking for a Titus 2 woman. Would you be the one?"

"Titus 2 woman" is code for "older woman." A euphemism for waning, fading, ancient woman. Me? How were we different? We both taught high school students. We both had children at the same school. We both had a youthful, current fashion sense. We were sisters, remember. I gathered myself and responded with a smile, "After I recover from the thought of being an older woman, we can talk about it."

The apostle Paul didn't have a thesaurus, apparently. He might have replaced "older" with elder, mature, grown, or senior. Just a better ring to it. Or maybe "women of a certain age" would be a lovely, vague option. OK, deal with it. I was older.

My life was forever changed. She and her friends called themselves "Excellent Wives." They didn't just want to study or know the Bible; they wanted it to change them. They were an accountability group of precious spirits. Just as Jesus taught the masses, discipled the Twelve, and focused on three, Peter, James, and John, God had given me "Patricia, Jaimie, and Joanne" to shepherd. I was not a mentor or teacher; too lofty. Just a candid, "what you see is what you get," flawed, wounded, caring friend with additional life experience. Ha!

> **They didn't just want to study or know the Bible; they wanted it to change them.**

Paul's letter to Titus not only exhorts older women to teach younger women, but to model Christ-like behavior. And he gives the reason: "That the Word of God may not be blasphemed." Paul wanted their lives and their actions to glorify God and strengthen the family. By doing so, God's reputation would not be discredited, no one could speak evil of them, and the church would grow (see Titus 2:5, 8). We are charged to teach, train, show, declare, remind, insist, rebuke, and direct one another toward further faith and knowledge of the truth. Not because we are perfect or superior, "for we ourselves were once foolish and disobedient" (Titus 3:3). God's goodness and loving-kindness saved us, that we might be justified (see Titus 3:4-6).

After fifteen years, I am officially old. AARP, Social Security, Medicare, all of it. God has guided our little flock and our families through pregnancies, strong-willed children, prodigal children, menopause, surgeries, a kidney transplant, alcoholism, the injustices of our legal system, financial distress, weddings, retirement, grandchildren, and more. And they taught me about texting, TJ Maxx, and chocolate-covered coffee beans. Yay! What a blessed fellowship God has given us, all because I agreed, prematurely, to be "older."

With the additional fifteen years of wisdom, my class roomie is now mentoring my precious daughter-in-law. They are a perfect fit, as all of God's designs are. I rejoice that another generation is being trained up. My cup runneth over!

Today, instead of feeling inferior or ashamed about my age, I will celebrate the way my unique life

experiences enrich my ability to relate to others.

CHAPTER 17

The Grass Withers, and the Flower Fades (Aging Gratefully)

Looking in the mirror each morning, I can only sing, "Amazing grace, how sweet the sound. Come save a wretch like me. I once was blond, but now I'm white, and I can barely see!" It ain't pretty. My eyebrows are gone, but I now have hair on my chin. My neck is slack, and my tummy falls on my lap when I sit. I'm covered with skin tags, age spots, freckles, and moles. And that is just the short list!

Aging is a crime in our culture. Women, especially, are required to resort to smoke and mirrors, bells and whistles. Yet God says youth is vanity (see Ecclesiastes 11:10). Fortunately, a wise Christian taught me in my youth about appearance. If it affects your ministry or turns others away from Jesus, fix it. If not, you're good to go. What seemed like sound advice when I was young became a thorn in the flesh as my grass withered and my flower faded.

Aging is a crime in our culture.

"Vanity, thy name is woman," right? Paul knew this when he instructed Timothy and Titus to admonish women to adorn themselves modestly, and with good deeds and integrity. "She who is self-indulgent is dead even while she lives" (1 Tim. 5:6). And the Proverbs 31 women? No mention of her youth or beauty; only her good heart and good deeds. Strength and dignity are her clothing. "Charm is deceitful, beauty is vain, but a woman who fears the Lord shall be praised." Ouch!

I once observed an adorable three-year-old girl at church. Big eyes, silky blond hair, flawless skin. God's perfect creation. She chose her own outfit for church to make her feel even prettier: mismatched skirt and blouse, purple headband, pink sparkle tennis shoes, and bangle bracelets of every color. Still beautiful and precious, but the add-ons looked so silly. And then I realized that's how I look to God when I add unnecessary adornments. Still a precious child in his sight, but silly.

"For the Lord sees not as man sees; man looks on the outward appearance, but the Lord looks on the heart" (1 Sam. 16:7). "God's delight is not in the strength of horses, nor his pleasure in the legs of man; but the Lord takes pleasure in those that fear him, in those who hope in his steadfast love" (Ps. 147: 10–11). God does not see cellulite or varicose veins. He does not see crepe-y skin and baggy knees. He does not take pleasure or delight in "thigh gap." God sees the heart and treasures those who fear him and find their hope in Him.

I smell smoke. The cult of youth is a lie from hell. The Father of Lies promotes pride and arrogance, but the Word of God says they are evil (see Proverbs 8:13). God opposes the proud and exalts the humble (see James 4:6). The boastful pride of life is of this world, but the world passes away (see John 2:16). Let's stop rearranging deck chairs on the Titanic.

The ship is going down no matter what we do! Yes, the grass withers and the flower fades, but the Word of the Lord stands forever (see Isaiah 40:8). "Look to him and be radiant, so your faces will never be ashamed" (Ps. 34:5). The Holy Spirit doesn't age! Don't just age gracefully; age *gratefully*. Be happy, and sow joy! Focus on what is blooming in your life, not what has withered.

> # Focus on what is blooming in your life, not what has withered.

I have decided to be what I am: a vintage, custom-made 1951 classic with all original parts. Priceless! I have indulged in a paint job. A touch of makeup for my fading face, and my once naturally blond hair now comes from a bottle. The grass continues to wither, but no BOTOX®, no implants, no cosmetic surgery, no fake nails. I'm grateful my engine still runs. As Indiana Jones says, "It's not the years; it's the mileage."

"Here is the conclusion of the matter: Fear God and keep His commandments, for this is the whole duty of man" (Eccles. 12:13).

Today I will focus less on the fleeting features of youth and fix my eyes instead on my eternal home with God in heaven.

CHAPTER 18

Surprise!
(Not What I Had Planned)

Early retirement. Surprise! Didn't like it. Didn't want it. Just as Jesus sent His disciples into stormy waters, He allowed the perfect storm of people and circumstances to rock my boat. And, like the disciples, I cried out, "Lord, do you not care?" Why should I leave the job I love? Make them leave! It did not happen. I was sunk.

So, what to do now? I did not want to be bored or boring. Maybe a substitute teacher. Maybe restart my tutoring business. Tennis and movies with friends? Surprise! My heart was planning my way, but God was directing my steps. Without warning, God unfolded my path. A young mother with three special-needs boys under the age of two desperately needed help. Really, Lord? I barely survived raising my own three boys. And I was younger then! Hmmmm. Thy will be done.

My mission: to bring glad tidings, heal the brokenhearted, release the captives, comfort, console, and bring beauty from ashes (Isa. 61). While The Mommy spent her days attached to a breast pump, I helped her with housework, groceries, laundry, bottle time, diaper time, nap time, and play time, sustained by Diet Coke, chocolate, and Red Vines. This was not my retirement vision. We were in the trenches, but it was my joy. What I thought would last six months continues today after ten years. Such a blessing.

God's Word is full of surprises and stunning transformations late in life. The gift of old age allows freedom, perspective, and toughness. Moses and Abraham were well prepared to be used by God. It is never too late to be great. Elizabeth was "advanced in years" when she conceived John, and she was the first to recognize Jesus. She exclaimed in a loud voice that

God had shown her favor. I echo her sentiment. Anna was "very old," living a simple life of prayer, worship, and service to others when God allowed her to recognize the Son of God when He was six weeks old. Her faithfulness was rewarded. Naomi lost her husband and sons, yet she remained kind, loving, and loyal as she faced her uncertain future. God showed up and showed off!

It has been said that old age is not for sissies. Amen! My body notifies me of declining strength and youth, and my mirror confirms it daily. This old gray mare ain't what she used to be! Yet I am determined to be open and available, letting God direct my steps. Thankfully, those who wait on the Lord renew their strength. They can run after toddlers and not grow weary. God has brought new people and projects I care deeply about. I want to invest myself in tomorrow and eternity. Naomi mentored Ruth, and Elizabeth mentored Mary. In our hectic, chaotic world, an older friend, advisor, confidant, and prayerful intercessor is a rare treasure. Forgetting what lies behind and reaching for those things that

> Those who wait on the Lord renew their strength.

lie ahead, I press on for the upward call of Jesus Christ. (Phil. 3:13–14).

Today, if something happens that was not in my plans or that disappoints me, I will open my heart and mind to see the path God wants me to follow.

CHAPTER 19

Ezra Called (The Gift of Time)

I am sixty-five years old. I have no problem with that. Empty nest, retirement, Social Security, Medicare, senior discounts. What's not to like? Others now have lower expectations of me. Yippee! Such freedom. My wardrobe does not need to be current. My mind does not need to be sharp. I do not need to be a techie. No need to do yoga or Pilates. Little is expected. If I do any of those things, I am met with surprise. Patronized, even. "Isn't she cute?" "What do you know?" "Good for you!"

However, my eldest son is turning forty. I *do* have a problem with that. How did *that* happen?

Then Ezra called. After seventy years and three generations, Israel had become soft and comfortable. God sent Ezra to stir things up. Shoot. Many of my friends and family members are sixty-five to seventy-plus years old. With grandchildren, we are now three generations. Maybe there is something to hear about this.

Leisure does not mean lazy.

Israel had forgotten God's promise, lost His vision, lost His calling. They had returned to old traditions and worshiped other gods. After seventy years, why not? They had suffered, battled, waited, and served long enough. It was *ME* time. They earned it, right?

But leisure does not mean lazy. Retirement is not meant for slouching into mediocrity. Freedom doesn't justify selfishness or indulgence; it opens doors to continue His calling. We are responsible to God for our gift of time. We have a stewardship responsibility to live productively. We are meant to be active partners in His work. Spend more time in His Word. More time in prayer. More time in His Presence.

Oh, Ezra. Maybe you have a wrong number? I think we have a bad connection. Are you saying put down the remote? And the golf clubs? Turn off my computer? Cancel the Spa Day? Cast out those idols? Confess, repent, and renew the covenant? Ask God to stir my spirit and direct my steps?

What did you say about Caleb? At eighty-five, his best years were ahead of him? He left a great inheritance because "he wholly followed God?" (Josh. 14:14).

Thanks for calling, Ezra. It is my privilege and my duty to wholly follow God *all* the days of my life. Eye has not seen, nor ear heard, neither has it entered the mind of man the wonderful things God has planned for those who love him (see 1 Corinthians 2:9).

Today, regardless of my age, I will declare, "The best is yet to come!" and continue to work for His good until I take my last breath.

CHAPTER 20

The Hooks and Eyes
(Keep Sewing)

My high school besties could sew. Their mothers sewed and passed that love and life skill on to them. Ever the follower, I was happy to go along. Soon, I learned about Butterick, Simplicity, and McCall patterns. I loved to use the little tracing-wheel tool. Thread the machine, wind the bobbin, cut the fabric, pin the pieces together. "Sew" much fun. A new skill, new clothes, and time with friends. We ate barrels of Chips Ahoy cookies as we worked. What could be better?

But there was more to learn. Some new sewers don't like doing darts or zippers. No problem. I had my seam ripper handy, and I could always have a "do-over." While I loved the big projects, I hated the final details. I was enthusiastic and energetic right up to the hem and the final hook and eye. Then my interest waned. The thrill was gone. Would someone else do these for me, please? I wanted the pleasure and reward of a new garment, but I didn't want to see it through to the end. Nevertheless, I gained the discipline to do it.

> God lifted my head to remind me that my life project was for life!

Such is life. In younger days, my time was filled with friends raising their children alongside me. Car pools, play groups, team moms, homeroom moms. I was inspired and invigorated by them, learning and trying new things, and eating chocolate delights to ward off fatigue and PMS. We enjoyed doing our "big project," child rearing, together. Gradually, though, those with fewer children or older children finished before me. Sadly, friends moved away or went back to work. I was left to do the hooks and eyes by myself. Total bummer. I pressed on to complete my work.

In time, I had my empty nest, and my teaching career ended. The big projects of my life were over. Time for little, self-indulgent projects? Just some peaceful downtime? No, wait. God lifted my head to remind me that my life project was for *life*! For *all* the days of my life, as He had planned before my birth (see Psalm 139:16 and Job 14:5). There is still hemming to do in my marriage and the hooks and eyes of other relationships to complete.

We are charged to do all of our work mightily. And whatever tasks we find to do should be done with all our hearts, as serving the Lord (see Ecclesiastes 9:10 and Colossians 3:23). No apathy. We are to conduct ourselves wisely, making the most of our time (see Colossians 4:5). God has not mended me just to be back on a hanger in the closet. He will increase the strength of my soul (see Psalm 138:3), giving me the will and the way to achieve His purposes.

God has filled my mouth with laughter and given me joy. He has done great things for me (see Psalm 126:2–3). "Let the redeemed of the Lord say so, whom He has redeemed from trouble" (Ps. 107:2). Whether it is another large, surprising project or just a bit of hemming, Lord, let me live that I might praise Thee (see Psalm 119:175).

Today I will consider the value in everything I do—not just the big projects but the smaller, more mundane tasks as well.

About the Author

Debbie Woods identifies with Gideon as "the least in my clan." After a traumatic teenage pregnancy, she was salvaged and rewoven by the Master Tailor, Jesus. His perfect redesign allowed a high school dropout to become a Spanish teacher who traveled, studied, and lived abroad, and a school board member.

During her teaching years, Debbie also led and assisted high school students on Mexico mission trips and European study trips. She supervised more than fifty students annually in her Spanish Club activities and was honored to be named to Who's Who Among American Teachers five times.

In retirement, Debbie became "The CraPft Queen," creating altered items that are "more crap than craft." Her focus is on blessing others, not artistic perfection. She and her husband, Tom, have three sons and four grandchildren.

IF YOU'RE A FAN OF THIS BOOK, PLEASE TELL OTHERS

If you believe in the message of this book and would like to share in the ministry of getting this important message out, please consider taking part by:

❑ Writing about it on your blog, Twitter, Facebook, and LinkedIn pages.

❑ Suggesting it to friends.

❑ Write a positive review on www.amazon.com.

❑ Send my publisher, HigherLife Publishing (media@ahigherlife. com), suggestions about websites, conferences, and events you know of where this book could be offered.

❑ Purchase additional copies to give away as gifts.

❑ You may contact Debbie at mendeddebbie2016@gmail.com.